SPANISH JOHN

Being a narrative of the Early Life of

Colonel John M'Donell
of Scottos

Written by himself

Illustrations by Anthea Craigmyle

Printed by Kelso Graphics, 1993.

Preface to the Present Edition

The 1931 edition of Spanish John's narrative of his early life is now a rarity, and a reprinting seems desirable. We are obliged to Major John MacDonald of Tote and Mr David Marriot, Inverie, for lending us their copies from which we and the printers have worked.

The narration has not been altered in this edition, though a few corrections have been made and the story has been divided into Chapters, for easier reading. Similarly, the notes are just as they were in the 1931 edition, save for the addition of a footnote to note 31. The illustrations are the only new feature.

The population of Knoydart in the 18th century was nearly 1,000 souls: today there are fewer than 100 living there, of whom very few have lived there all their lives. There being no roads into the hinterland the district is very much isolated. The nearest town of any size is Mallaig, which did not exist in Spanish John's time, and that is more than 5 miles by sea from Inverie pier.

We are obliged to Miss Mary Hill, Schoolteacher at Inverie, for reminding us of how it is that the name of Spanish John is still surprisingly well-known in the West Highlands. She writes:-

> *The reprinting of the autobiography of Colonel John MacDonnell of Scottas will bring his exploits to a wider public and explain the strange name of a boat that plies the Western sea-boards of Lochaber.*

Preface to the Present Edition

The children of Knoydart today still have to leave home at the age of 12 to continue their education, but only to, to them, the far-off towns of Fort William and Portree. Not for them the sailing ship or the "coach d'eau" nor indeed rescue by a Spanish Zebec. The present day children are conveyed by Cal-Mac or by the Knoydart Estate landing craft "Spanish John".

The name and the story of Spanish John remain, for us in Knoydart, a part of our everyday life two hundred and fifty years later, thanks to the naming of this craft, which I have always felt was inspired.

Scottas House is not as Spanish John would have remembered it, for it was reconstructed some years after he emigrated, but the fact that it is still a dwelling house gives a sense of continuity with the past, something which is sadly lacking in so many areas of Highland life today.

Craigmyle
Scottas House
Knoydart
June 1993

Preface to the 1931 Edition

The attention of the Society was drawn to these reminiscences of Colonel John Macdonell, popularly known as Spanish John, by one of its members, the Rev. Andrew MacDonell, O.S.B., M.C.

Colonel Macdonell was born at Scottos or Scotus in Knoydart in 1728. In 1773 he left Scotland for America. During the War of Independence he fought in the British Army, and after its conclusion settled in Canada. He died on 15th April 1810.

A good deal of information regarding his life in America and his family is given by the Rev. A.G. Morice, O.M.I., in the Canadian 'Historical Review' for September and December 1929.

Some time before his death he wrote this account of his early life at the request and for the information of his own family. In April and May 1825 it appeared in the 'Canadian Magazine,' a periodical published in Montreal. That magazine is now extremely rare, and no copy is believed to exist in this country.

Intensely interesting as a tale of adventure, Colonel Macdonell's narrative also throws fresh light on the evil days that followed Culloden, while the writer is himself such a fine example of the Highland gentleman that the Council gladly acceded to the suggestion of Father MacDonell that it should be printed from a transcript which he had the kindness to offer for that purpose.

Although this autobiography itself has never been reprinted, it has been made use of in other ways. In 1898 there appeared a novel entitled 'Spanish John,' by William MacLennan. It contains numerous conversations and descriptions of scenery, and sundry imaginary characters appear in its pages, but otherwise it is just this autobiography. So far as appears there is no reference to the source of the writer's inspiration, and the ordinary reader might well be excused for regarding the book as an attempt to emulate Mr R.L. Stevenson.

Preface to the 1931 Edition

Mr William MacLennan was followed by Mr Andrew Lang, who, in July 1898, contributed to 'Macmillan's Magazine' an article on Colonel Macdonell's 'Memoirs' which he says appeared in the 'Canadian Magazine' of July 1828 (*sic*). It is in the ordinary style affected by that writer when dealing with Highland matters, and he gave it a title which was gratuitously offensive. Some little time previously Mr Lang had published a book in which he sought to identify a Hanoverian spy known as *Pickle* with Alastair Ruadh, the chief of Glengarry, whom he accordingly represented as a singularly infamous person. In view of the fact that Glengarry and Spanish John were near of kin, Mr Lang thought proper to entitle his article "A Cousin of Pickle."

What the authors of 'Clan Donald' thought of Mr Lang and his methods is frankly stated in various passages of their work. And some prudent friend may have pointed out that such a description of Colonel Macdonell might possibly provoke reprisals in kind from other people aggrieved by Mr Lang's habitual attitude to all things Highland – reprisals which in his case would be highly relevant and far from pleasant. But be this as it may, when reprinted with other articles in a miscellany volume it received the more seemly title "A Gentleman of Knoydart."

A few notes have been added, chiefly to identify persons mentioned or as illustrating the accuracy of the narrative. Those enclosed in square brackets appeared in the 'Canadian Magazine,' and some of them appear to have been added to his MS. by the author himself.

For the portrait of Spanish John, done after his removal to America, the Society is further indebted to the kindness of Father MacDonell.

J.R.N.M.

Chapter 1

Journey to Rome

Dear Sir – Urged by your earnest desire of having a short sketch of my early life, although there are no very extraordinary events, or indeed anything entertaining in it to an indifferent person, and you know very well that I am only capable of relating things as they fell out without any embellishment, – you shall have as much as I at this distant period of time can recollect, and in as succinct a manner as I possibly can.

In the year 1740, my father thought proper to send me to the Scotch College at Rome for my education, where he had been educated himself, and I believe with a view of making a Clergyman of me: Yet he told me at taking leave, that he did

I left the Highlands

Chapter 1

not mean to force my inclination, and that I might act as I thought proper when I (should come) of years sufficient to form a notion of what would suit my own fancy best.

I left the Highlands some time in August, accompanied by a young lad of the family of Clanronald, Angus McDonald by name, intended likewise by his parents for a Clergyman of the Church of Rome. Arrived at Edinburgh, we had recommendations to a Bishop Hay in that city, where we staid seven or eight weeks waiting for a passage to Boulogne in France. Bishop Hay took great care of us, and told the Capt. of the ship to use us in the best manner, and gave us letters of recommendation to one Mr. Hay, a wine merchant at Boulogne, to whom he also wrote to have us sent to Paris without loss of time, to the care of one Mr. George Innis the Superior of the Scotch College at Paris ([1]). From Boulogne we took our journey in the stage coach, the hire of which and passage on ship-board was previously paid for us; we only paid for our eating and drinking, which, by and bye, we found troublesome enough;– The Inn keepers in France are mostly as in other parts of the world, very apt to impose on strangers, particularly such as come from our country, and unfortunately for us, neither my comrade or I knew a word of French. We made, however, the best shift we could. The coach carried us to that city, and the good Mr. Innes had a person in waiting at the tavern where the coach put up, who brought us in a hackney coach to his College, where we were used as the children of the House for four or five weeks, the time of our stay at Paris.

On leaving Paris we embarked in what is called there a Coach d'Eau; went up the Seine River as far as Auxerre, where we took a Caleche as far as Chalons upon the Seine River, and again embarked in the Coach d'Eau, for the city of Lyons. And from thence went by land in a Caleche as far as Avignon, where we waited on the Popes Legat, who governed there for his Holiness ([2]). Staid at Avignon two days, then proceeded in a caleche to Marseilles. (Please to observe that our carriage by land and water was all paid for us, and that we were recommended from one place to another and supplied with money to pay our tavern expences at every city we came to, where we had orders to draw money from bankers of our own nation then established in the different cities.)

At Marseilles, being to embark for Italy, we took up as much money as would defray our expences by land and water to Rome, and then went on board of a ship bound for Leghorn. There were on board some passengers of different nations, viz. an Italian Count and his Lady, a Spanish traveller also bound for Leghorn, and a tall Irish fellow named O'Rourk, from the county of Tipperary, who was going to finish his studies at the Propaganda Fidei at Rome.

A tall Irish fellow named O'Rourk

Chapter 1

Set sail, but were at night overtaken by such a heavy storm as drove us into Toulon, where we were very glad to come to anchor in the midst of the French fleet lying then in that harbour.

We wanted next day to go on shore, but it blew very hard, and luckily we got frightened and desisted. The sailors, however, got some of the ship's guns put into the boat, by way of ballast, and six of the men and the ships cook, who immediately took the helm, and a French cordeliere friar ([3]) got into the boat; on putting off from the ship both sails were scarcely filled when by some mismanagement the boat overset, all hands, priest and all got up on her keel and were thus driving fast into the offing and must have gone out to sea, had not a Spanish Zebec, then in the harbour, made sail, and saved the men – the boat went out to sea. Our captain went next day ashore and bought another boat, in which my comrade and I thought proper to go and see the town of Toulon. We repeated this exercise every day for several days, I remained sometimes to a late hour in the town.

One night as we walked through the streets and cracking nuts, my comrade who was somewhat roguish, (playful), observed a Monsieur with a large powdered wig, and his hat under his arm, going past us; he took a handul of nuts from his pocket and threw them with all his force at the Frenchman's head, which unfortunately disordered his wig. Monsieur turned upon and collered him; by good luck the Spaniard was of our party, who instantly ran to the relief of my comrade and gave the Frenchman a severe drubbing. We then adjourned to a tavern, when our Spaniard calling for a bottle of wine, brought me to a private room, and after bolting the door, to my great terror and surprise, drew (a large knife) a stilletto with his right hand from his left bosom, made me understand by signs that with that weapon he would have killed the Frenchman if he had proved too strong for him. He then took a net purse out of his pocket wherein there appeared to be about

Journey to Rome

Monsieur turned upon and collered him

a hundred Spanish pistoles, and made me an offer of a part; I made him a low bow, but not standing in need of it, would not accept of his liberality, for I thought I had enough being always purse bearer for myself and companion. – My friend made sometimes free with my pockets, merely to try if I should miss any thing, and was happy to find that I made a discovery of his tricks by immediately missing what he took in that way. I bought out of our stock two large folding French knives, by way of carvers, in case of any sinister accident, one of which each had in his pocket.

Chapter 1

After a tedious though pleasant passage we arrived at Leghorn, where we parted with our Italian and Spanish passengers; but to our great mortification and disappointment, the little french we had picked up in our way through France was of no manner of service to us in Italy, and we had not a word of Italian, and no Latin except what our Tipperary gentleman spoke. By means of O'Rourk we were informed that two Scottish gentlemen who were making the grand tour were then at Leghorn, on whom we all then waited to pay them our respects. It being in the evening, these gentlemen invited us all to breakfast with them the next morning. We went accordingly. Our Hibernian at breakfast got hold of the teapot to help us to some tea, and at the very first motion spilt a tea cupful of that liquor on the calf of the leg of a Mr. Ramsay, one of the two gentlemen travellers who had invited us, upon which he started up and took a pretty good dance

dance through the room without any music

through the room without any music. The next day we procured an Interpreter by means of whom we hired a Caleche to carry my comrade and me to Rome.

Set out for Rome came to a town the name of which I forget; the driver brought us to a good tavern, when to our great surprise we found our former fellow traveller, Mr. O'Rourk, and another decent man who he introduced by the name of Mr. Creach, formerly of the Irish regiments in Spain. O'Rourk and my comrade went to see the town while dinner was getting ready. Mr. Creach and I remained at the Inn. I was walking backward and forward in the room when Mr Creach asked me if I would lend him some money. I answered that I was quite a stranger in the country, had no friends, and was afraid I should run short before coming to the end of my journey, and of course could spare none. "You little puppy," says Creach, "I will have it whether you will or not," at the same time he seized me by the collar; I, as quick as lightning, closed with him, and we had a smart struggle. I was afraid that the fellow would overpower me, but in the nick of time my comrade coming up stairs and seeing my danger, seized Creach by one leg – I was instantly on the top of him, laid both my knees upon his arms, sat upon his breast, and drew my big French couteau to cut his throat, which I certainly would have accomplished, had not O'Rourk appeared, who cried out, "Do not kill him, but as I can speak Latin, I will go to the Magistrates and get him put into prison!" Very well, I returned, call the land-lord to take care of him. I left him there and never more heard of him.

O'Rourk told me that he understood by the natives that a wood which lay in our way was much frequented by Robbers, upon which I thought proper to purchase a pair of pistols; and after loading them, gave one to my comrade, McDonald, telling him that we must fight for our lives if we were attacked, to which he cheerfully assented. We were, however, quite without fear; lodged that night at Viterbo, a town about

Chapter 1

forty miles from Rome. Next day got to Rome, and to my great surprise my adventure with Creach, the purchase of the pistols along with my resolute behaviour, had got to the city before my arrival. It was looked upon of course as a prodigy that two young boys, my comrade of fourteen years of age, and I of twelve, could have strength and resolution to go through such an adventure with success. It was afterwards of service to me when I left College to go to the army. My leaving the College renewed in the memory of my countrymen then at Rome, my former behaviour on my way to that city.

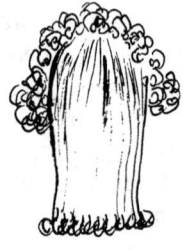 

Chapter 2

Into College and Out

I was upon my arrival at Rome, admitted into the Scotch College, after that the usual ceremonies of admittance were performed. An Italian nobleman, a Jesuit, was rector, who, to begin with our education, hired a private master to teach us some Italian and the rudiments of the Latin language. After this master had taught us for a couple of months we were sent to the public schools of the Roman College, where every science was taught by a number of Jesuits, learned, I may say, in every branch of education. Being the youngest boy in the College, I chanced to be the Superior's favorite – this encouraged me very much, and I resolved to do my utmost to merit it, and to please my benefactor and protectors to the utmost of my power so that in a short time I got the start of my Italian school fellows, who were pretty numerous, and I was consequently removed to a higher class, equally numerous with the one I came from.

Unfotunately for me there was a Maronite, a fellow from near Mount Libanus, very swarthy, who sat near me upon the uppermost Bench, and while school was in, either through weakness or some other cause, wetted the bench quite close to where I sat; and whispered to one near him that I had done it. Being forbid to speak in the school I waited patiently till the bell rang to dismiss the school for the time; upon the first toll of which I made for the school room door, stood by the side post to wait the coming out of the Maronite who had so grossly belied and affronted me. Upon his approach I gave him a blow as hard as I could strike about his upper lip and nose, which produced a copious discharge of blood. As fast as

Chapter 2

I could I ran and joined my fellow collegioners, who were not at all sorry for what I had done, and promised me protection as far as their interest could procure it.

The laws of the Roman College punished such offences with a very rigorous penalty; which was, that the person i.e., scholar guilty of raising his hand to strike another within the outer walls of the college, was to be put into the stocks, hand and feet, and to receive as many lashes with a cat o'-nine tails upon the back and shoulders, as should be thought proper, and laid on with a severity according to the nature of the offence. This punishment was called a Mule. Next to this for crimes less atrocious was a Horse. The operation of which was to stand upon a bucket stool, and to be flogged with a cat o'-nine tails on the small of the legs.

Soon after our return from school a message was sent to father Urbani, our Rector, giving an account of the crime committed by Little John Giovannini M'Donald, which was the name I went by. I was of course called for by the Superior in presence of my fellow collegioners and accused of my crime. Without hesitation I avowed my guilt, and I was then told by the Superior that I must undergo the punishment due to my crime. This I refused to comply with, and said that such punishments were unworthy of freeborn people. All my comrades joined me in remonstrances, and said that we would sooner leave the schools of the Roman College and go to the schools of the Propaganda College than to be subjected to such punishments. The result was that the rest of the Collegioners went to school as usual, and I was kept at home. As soon as my comrades had gone to school, the worthy Rector, Father Urbani, sent for me and asked me if I would accompany him in a coach to see some of the antiquities of Rome! I answered that I would go with him any where, but would never consent to receive a Mule or a Horse. "My dear little Johnny," says he, "I see you have a great deal of spirit; it must not be broke." In short, we continued our coach exercise for three days. The good Father being treated sumptuously wherever he called, I had a plentiful share, besides, he informed me of every particular relating to the antiquities we saw. At the three days end, he desired me to go to school, I answered that I would do any thing I was able, but to keep me clear of Mules and Horses. "You may, my dear child," said he, "they shall never be put to your offer." I went accordingly to school upon his word, and never heard anything more about the matter.

In the winter of 1743, Prince Charles Edward, eldest son of King James VIII of Scotland, commonly called the Pretender, went off privately from Rome in the habit of a Spanish courier for France, then at war with Great Britain. The opinion then prevalent in Rome, and indeed every where, was, that the French had encouraged him with promises of his restoration to the British Throne: which opinion set a great many people's heads and hands to work. Among the rest I began to think that probably my clan would not be the last to join the young Charles if a descent upon any part of Britain took place in his favour. I had read the history of the civil wars in the reigns of King Charles the I and II in which many gallant actions were performed by my predecessors and namesakes in the royal cause. This set my brains agoing, which were not very settled of themselves. I got disgusted with the life of a student, and thought I should be much happier in the army.

Without disclosing my sentiments to any one except my former friend and companion, Angus M'Donald, we set ourselves a scheming which way I might put my design in practice. There was a privilege which our students had above all other Colleges in Rome, which was, that any two of us might at certain hours go wherever our business called us. This liberty I thought proper to use in order to forward my plan. Angus M'Donald and myself went out together and waited on some noble-men of the Pretender's Court, to whom I declared my intention of leaving the gown, and taking the

Chapter 2

sword. Every one praised my spirit and promised to get me well recommended. At that very time there was a Spanish army in Italy ([4]) commanded by one Count de Gages, a Fleming by birth; next to him in command was a Lieutenant General M'Donell of the family of Antrim ([5]). There was likewise in this Spanish army an Irish Brigade, which originally was a part of the 14,000 men, that by capitulation ([6]), went to France along with King James II of England and VII of Scotland, when beaten out of Ireland by his son-in-law, King William. This brigade was afterwards sent to Spain by Louis the XIV of France, along with Philip V of Spain, and now were naturalised Spaniards, although all their officers were Irish, except one or two Scots. At the time alluded to, this Spanish army after a severe battle with the Austrians where both sides claimed the victory, had retired from the Modenese to winter quarters in the Pope's territories on the Adriatic coast, occupying the towns of Pezaro, Faro, &c., &c., in order to cover the Kingdom of Naples on that side, then governed by Charles, eldest son of Philip V and which was to be attacked in the spring by the Austrian army as soon as it could get reinforced, all of which followed.

By the help of this privilege of the College and the company of my friend M'Donald, I was introduced to King James by noblemen attending on that Prince, who enquired of me particularly about my grand-father and grand-uncles ([7]), with all of whom he had been acquainted personally in the year 1715. – A recommendation was soon made out for me directed to Lieut. Genl. M'Donell: – I then without loss of time made the Rector acquainted with my intentions of leaving the College. He very civily told me that he was sorry for it; and encouraged me very much to enter into the society of the Jesuits; this I declined with as good a grace as I could. When he found me inflexible, he brought me along with him in a coach to the Cardinal Protector; – and after that we had been both treated with chocolate and sugar biscuits, he informed the

Into College and Out

He very civilly told me he was sorry for it

Cardinal of my intentions. His Eminence asked me what I came to the college for, as it was a religious house founded by Pope Clement the VIII by way of resource for Catholic Clergy, when the Catholic religion was persecuted in Scotland, in the time of the reformation? I answered that I could not tell. He then spoke of the Bishops at home, finding fault with them for sending children abroad without knowing their inclination. I was very glad when we got away from him. My true friend the Rector then told me that I should be supplied by him with cloaths and money, and that I might go home to Scotland or wherever I pleased. I then freely opened my mind to this most worthy clergyman, and told him of my intentions of going to the army. "My dear little Johnny.' he

Chapter 2

..... next for a tailor ..... and without loss of time made me ready like a gentleman

said. "if you will go to the Queen of Hungary's service, I can get you strongly recommended to persons of the greatest interest." But, father, my inclination leads me to serve his Catholic Majesty, and his army is now not far off, and a number of British subjects are in that army, though, by the bye, as I mentioned above, they were all exiles. He sent me next for a tailor, a brocker, a periwig maker, &c., &c., and without loss of time made me ready like a gentleman; and presenting me with a sword, his eyes filled, and he told me that I should lose that sword by the enemy, which was verified in seven or eight months after.

Chapter 3

A Smell of Powder

I took a formal leave of all my friends and acquaintances at Rome; set out for the Spanish army in company with some young gentlemen volunteers who had come from the army to see that ancient city, in whose company I or any young lad, who after spending three years where vice was painted as black as it ought to be, would be shocked at all the vices they seemed by their conversation to be so full of. They even told me that I should be good for nothing until the silly notions I imbibed from a parcel of bigots, were removed: I however had no inclination to alter my own way of thinking; on the contrary I pitied them very much, and did not scruple to tell them so, but I might as well preach to the wind.

Arrived at Faro, being head quarters, I was presented to general M'Donnell by our Irish captain, and delivered my recommendations to his Excellency; the first injunction he laid upon me was to dine every day at his table. This of itself was forwarding me at once into public notice, as he was constantly surrounded by Spanish noblemen and most of the officers of note in the army, to whom he always introduced me as a young Scotch Highlander from the college of Rome, strongly recommended, and come to acquire some knowledge of military affairs. His son, Donald M'Donald, Colonel of the regiment Irelanda, entered me a Cadet in his own company. I was caressed by the Leiut. General, his son Donald, my Colonel and Captain, and by his brother Ronald, who was afterwards Colonel of the Regiment – and also by their uncle, Major Genl. M'Donnell, brother to the Lieut. Genl. who was allowed to be the best foot officer and engineer in Spain. –

Chapter 3

Every captain of Grenadiers or battalion belonging to the brigade when sent out on service, would have me for his companion during his turn of service, which when over, I always repaired to Genl. M'Donell, to whom I must in the most minute manner give an account of every transaction that happened in the command I was on.

Early in spring of 1744, our army marched along the Adriatic coast by Ancona, Loretto &c., to cover the kingdom of Naples on that side. The Austrian vanguard came to an action with our rear between Ancona and Loretto, which they

Spanish Grenadier

A Smell of Powder

pressed so hard upon that our people were giving way; upon which a reinforcement was ordered to support them – I chanced to be of the number; our people were in very bad order, retiring, and the enemy pursuing. Their balls whistling full in our ears, and they advancing almost upon a charge. Our reinforcement was advancing in high spirits and in good order; I'll tell you the truth, I felt myself rather queer, my heart panting very strong, not with bravery I assure you. I thought that every bullet would finish me, and thought seriously to run away, a cursed thought! I dare never see my friends or nearest relations after such dastardly conduct. My thoughts were all at once cut short by the word of command, advance quick. We were at once within about one hundred paces of the enemy, to whom we gave so well directed a fire that their impetuosity was bridled. The firing on both sides continued until dark came on, which put a stop to the work of the evening. The enemy retreated some distance back, and we rejoined our own army. I went to Genl. M'Donnell, who asked me if I had smelled powder to-day. I told him "I had plentifully," "what Sir," said he, "are you wounded?" "No, please your excellency," "Sir, you will never smell powder until you are wounded." I got great credit from the Officers commanding the party I belonged to, for my undaunted behaviour during the action, but they little knew what passed within me before it began.

Continued our route some days after, traversed the frontiers of Naples, until we covered the part bordering the Ecclesiastical state on the Mediterranean. Having got intelligence that the Austrian army consisting of forty-five thousand men, under the command of Prince Lobcowitz and the famous Genl. Brown ([8]), had changed its route in order to enter the kingdom of Naples on that side. We were joined by thirty thousand Neapolitan troops with their King, which made us at least equal in number to the Austrians. We encamped our whole army about the town of Viletri, in the Pope's territories; took possession of the heights above the town, which was

Chapter 3

scarcely done when a sharp action commenced between ours and the enemy's advanced parties. Out chief genls. commanded day about, count Gages one day, and Castro Pignani, the Neapolitan general, the next day; which of them commanded on that day I cannot affirm, but I think it was the Neapolitan, who thought proper to order the troops upon the heights, to abandon them, and to encamp near the rest of the army on the lower ground; a fatal error! – which occasioned in the end the destruction of almost both armies. By this unaccountable blunder the enemy had not only a full view of our army and position, but had likewise possession of the main road leading to Rome, and of the conduits by which the camp and town were chiefly supplied with water, which they cut off from us entirely, and erected batteries that constantly annoyed our advanced posts. Our main armies were not above four miles asunder; every day produced severe actions begun between our parties. Each army being near enough to send support to its own people. – These engagements continued generally till night coming on put an end to them; and were renewed every morning at day-break, when our people went to water their horses and mules at the cisterns and fountains dispersed over the country. This work continued some time; at last the enemy got so bold as to attack our out posts with such success as obliged our people to yield a part of the ground we had in possession, I chanced to be one of the number in this very hot affair.

Being sentry about an hour before day I was alarmed by hearing the trampling of Horses and stir of men advancing towards my post. I challenged, and was answered by Lieut. Genl. M'Donell, whose voice I knew, and he knowing mine, said, "Is that you M'Donell?" I answered in the affirmative; Get yourself relieved, and come with me." While the relief was coming I asked, he halting, where is your Excellency going, "To beat those rascals from their advantageous posts," I instantly got relieved and joined. The first battery we attacked was of four 18 pounders, which, after receiving one discharge from it was carried, and 300 men made prisoners. After getting possession of this battery it could not long be maintained, being exposed to and commanded by the posts from the heights, namely Monte Artemisio and Monte Cucu. The Lieut. Genl. hesitated not a minute to take his resolution, and forming the army he commanded into three Columns, attacked the highest, which was Monte Artemisio, which was carried in two hours time, with some loss of men.

The troops on Monte Cucu being something lower and partly commanded by the other, the enemy abandoned it and retreated to their camp, which we then had a full view of, and seemed to be in great confusion. The Lieut. Genl. poured down from the heights with his columns, at sight of which the enemy left their camp and took post in a wood in the rear of it. At this juncture M'Donell received peremptory orders, by an Aide-de-Camp to retreat, which he obeyed, after setting what he could of the enemy's camp on fire, but he prayed heartily for the commanding Generals and their orders. Monte Cucu being the lowest of the two was abandoned, but he ordered strong batteries and posts to be erected on Monte Artemisio and returned to camp. He had been ordered only to attack and take the first battery of guns; and finding that commanded by the other two hills, he attacked them without waiting for further orders, he said that he would send all the enemy's army to Old Nick, had he been allowed to go on his own way. – The King approved very much of M'Donell's conduct, and to cover him, said the he had acted by his orders. Monte Cucu was immediately taken possession of by the enemy and fortified in the strongest manner, from which we were not able in spite of all our endeavours to dislodge them during the rest of the campaign. Major Genl. M'Donell had the charge of fortifying Monte Artemisio and its dependencies.

The armies remained in their respective camps, I cannot say inactive, for not a day passed without obstinate and very

Chapter 3

bloody skirmishes. At length the Austrian General, Prince Lobcowitz, formed a scheme to surprise our army and make the King of Naples prisoner for which purpose he was marching and counter marching his army for several days to deceive us, by seeming to provide for a retreat as the Austrian army by the sword and sickness was reduced at least a third in number more than ours. The sick and wounded he sent off in waggons to a great distance from his camp.

On the 11th of August a most furious and determined attack was made upon our strong posts and camp. The camp was to have been attacked a little before day break by three columns of regular troops preceded by the Croats, Pandours, and Talpatihes, the irregulars of the army; all under the command of the celebrated Marshal Brown, who was afterwards killed by the Prussians at the battle of Prague in Bohemia. Our out posts

Spanish light horse

A Smell of Powder

were always relieved before day, the weather being very hot. Having been warned the preceding evening for guard, I threw myself down in a shade that had been prepared for Divine service, to take a few hours rest with my clothes on, accompanied by a young fellow come piping-hot from Ireland to enter himself a Cadet in our Regiment. I cannot as yet imagine what was the cause of my not being called to that guard in proper time. I awoke a little before day-break; heard two shots, then half a dozen, next a couple of vollies, when starting up, I told my guest that we were certainly attacked. What shall I do, he says, I have no arms. I told him to fall into the ranks, and that if he was killed in the first fire he'd have no occasion for any, and that if he survived he would get as many as he pleased. But says he I have not yet been reviewed! I told him that ten to one he never would, but that I must go. I ran as fast as I could to the piquet, called to the Drummer to beat the General, which was instantly repeated by all the drums in the army.

The men ran to their arms and formed, some clothed, some half clothed, and some in their shirts. Our brigade in their encampment faced the town; there was unfortunately one or two regiments of Horse encamped in our rear, who, not having time to saddle their Horses, broke through our brigade before we were half formed, being pursued by the enemy's irregulars whose advance was put a stop to by some volleys from our two Irish Regiments. A Regiment of Petite Walloons that had been added to us to complete our brigade which was to have consisted of six battalions, gave way, and was followed by a great body of cowardly Neapolitans, which cut off our poor battalion from the rest of our line, Count Brown taking immediately possession of the abandoned ground. By fronting the enemy our right became our left where there was an impassable ravine, the enemy's irregulars in front, supported by a body of regulars; so that being attacked in front and flanked on our right, we retreated after leaving a good part of our Officers and men on the field.

Chapter 3

For my own share I was among the last that gave way, but when I once turned my back I imagined the enemy all aimed at me alone, and therefore ran with all my might, and thought there was a weight tied to each of my legs, till I had out run every one, and looking behind saw the whole coming up. I halted and faced about, every one as he came up did the same, we soon formed a regular line and resolved to revenge our dead comrades and to fight to the last, but found our situation to be as bad as before. We wheeled to the right to endeavour to enter the town by the nearest gate in order to defend ourselves there by the help of an old Roman wall that surrounded the town; but the guard at the gate and those upon the wall fired upon us, mistaking us for the enemy, and a column of Brown's men coming up gave us another fire. To extricate ourselves from this very critical situation, we made a wheel to the left to recover our former ground, which with great loss we accomplished, but with still as bad, if not worse chance, than before, for a body of the enemy got between us and the ravine, by which means we were attacked on both flanks and in front.

Reduced to extremity, we offered to capitulate upon Honorable terms, but could obtain no condition except surrendering at discretion, rather than which we resolved to fight while powder and ball remained among the living or the dead. A French Major Genl. who commanded us, was killed. Our Colonel Donald M'Donnel, advanced two or three paces to see if we could open a passage with our bayonets, was shot through with seven balls [9]. Our Officers and men fell very fast. I among the rest got a ball through my thigh which prevented my standing; I crossed my firelock under my thigh and shook it to try if the bone was whole, which finding to be the case, dropt on the one knee and continued firing. I received another shot which threw me down. I made once more an attempt to help my surviving comrades, but received a third wound which quite disabled me. Loss of blood, and no way to stop it, soon reduced my strength, I however gripped my sword to be ready to run through the first enemy that should insult me.

All our ammunition being spent, not a single cartridge remained amongst the living or the dead, quarters were called for by the few that were yet alive. Many of the wounded were knocked on the head: – and I did not escape with impunity; one approached me. At first, I made ready to run him through, but observing five or more close to him, I dropt the sword, and was saluted with Hunts foot ([10]). Accompanied with a cracking of Muskets about my head, I was only sensible of three blows and fainted; I suppose they thought me dead. On coming to myself again I found my clothes were stripped off, weltering in my blood and no one alive near me to speak to – twisting and rolling in the dust with pain, and my skin scorched by the sun. In this condition a Croat came up to me with a cocked pistol in his hand, asked for my purse in bad Italian. I told him that I had no place to hide it in, and if he found it any where about me, to take it. "Is that an answer for me you son of a b——ch," at the same time pointing his pistol straight between my eyes. I saw no one near, but the word quarter was scarcely expressed by me, when I saw his pistol arm seized by a genteel young man dressed only in his waistcoat, who said to him, you rascal let the man die as he pleases, you see he had enough, go and kill some one able to resist ([11]) – the fellow went off. Pray Sir said I to the young man, what do you mean to make of this town if you take it? "to keep it if we can, if not to burn it.' I asked if he could get me brought to their camp to have my wounds dressed, that I would reward him with fifty guinies. He disappeared for a few minutes and came back with four stout German soldiers, to whom he spoke something in their language, when they seized me by the arms and legs to carry me away; no sooner was my head removed from the ground than I fainted, and on recovering, found myself where I formerly was. The young man was yet near, who told me that I could not be removed. Sir, said I to him, If you set the town

Chapter 3

on fire I shall infallibly be burnt here! "If I am alive," he returned, "I will prevent that: in the meantime I must attend to my duty, for the firing in the streets continues very hot," with that he left me, and I saw no more of him (12).

I observed a regiment of horse drawn up about half a gun shot from where I lay, the sight of which drew my attention. They faced the town, and if they advanced a few paces more I was afraid they would crush me under their feet. They faced to the rear, retired a little way and then faced the town again. This manoeuvring surprised me, I listened attentively and heard the cannon and platoons approach, I raised my head supported on my hand, and looked earnestly at the nearest gate to me, which was quite full of men running out and trailing their arms. They soon formed a line between me and the horse already mentioned. The distance between my enemies and friends was so small, and my sight so weak that I could not distinguish the one from the other, till I observed our people forming a line opposite to the other between me and the town wall. I looked upon myself then as certain of death, but still using all the precaution in my power to preserve life, I seized two of my dead comrades by the collar, who lay thick enough round me, and with great difficulty dragged myself so as to

raised my head on my hand and looked earnestly

have a corpse on each side, to save me from the straggling balls of each line. I did not remain long in this danger, for the enemy at the second fire from our people left their ground and fled out of sight. I called to every one I could speak to for a drink, but from the heat of the day and length of the action their canteens and calebashes were all emptied. At last I saw a Grenadier of the Swiss guards whose uniform was very much like ours, with a large calabash; asked him if he had any thing in it, he said he had; will you let me have a drink? yes brother, said he, mistaking me I suppose for a Swiss. I took a hearty draught of excellent wine, then offered it back to him. No, no, brother, said he, I am unhurt and you cannot help yourself; with that he left me. There was one Lieut. Buttler of ours lying near me upon all fours, who I did not before observe; he begged in the name of God to let him have a drink; I drew myself a little nearer to him, for he could not stir, and handed him the calebash; he would have certainly finished the contents, but observing the liquor mixt with his blood come through him as fast as he drank it, I pulled the calebash from him, telling him that in all likelihood his bread was baked, and it would be unfair in him to swallow my drink without benefit, and let me perish for want of it. I remained in this situation till towards evening, when Miles M'Donnell then a Lieutenant in Hebernia's Regt. who had that day been on some distant guard, came to view the destruction of his countrymen, and to know whether I was dead or a prisoner, found me and got me carried on the leaf of a door, to the bloody hospital, saw my wounds dressed and reported my condition to Lieut. Genl. M'Donnell.

Chapter 4

A Second Campaign

Ronald, the only surviving son of Lieut. Genl. M'Donell was promoted by the King of Naples, (who joined himself in the late action to the Lieut. Genl.) to be Colonel of our regiment in place of his elder brother killed as already related. – He came to the Hospital twice a day, morning and evening by particular orders from his father, to see me ([13]). In about six weeks I began to go upon crutches, and in a few days more went to the Lieut. Genls quarters. When cured of my wounds I had no clothes, not even a shirt. The General sent me a suit of his own clothes and half a dozen of shirts; and in a letter he wrote to King James, giving an account of the late battle, his own loss in the death of his son, without my knowledge, mentioned my situation to His Majesty who was pleased to order a pretty good sum of money for my immediate occasions. – I was afraid to meet the General as a sight of me might renew his grief for the loss of his son, but he was a true soldier and showed me an example of fortitude by saying in a jocose manner, "are you still alive?" "I hope your Excellency has sent no person to kill me," "By G–d, I thought you had enough but I know what brought you here today, you come for a good dinner after being starved in Hospital; but be very careful, I have seen a great many that killed themselves in the same manner; they eat more than they can degest, then get a flux and off they go;" "I hope that will not be my case" I replied. Dinner was served up at the usual time; I sat at table nearly opposite to the Genl. who eyed me from time to time; at last he got up, took my knife and fork from me, ordered away what was before me, said "you D–l, you'll kill yourself;" I believe I should have ran some risk had he not prevented me.

About the end of September the Austrian army retreated, reduced in number to not more than ten thousand men, and followed as was said by 12,000 women. We pursued them next day with an army also much reduced in number, and expected to bring them to action at Torre Metia, or half way town between Albano and the city of Rome, which was the route they took. Both armies had engaged to his Holiness not to enter Rome. The enemy marched round the walls and our advanced guard coming up to their rear under the walls, a pretty warm skirmish began between them and continued till the enemy crossed the Milvian Bridge, where the tyrant Maxentius was drowned by Constantine the Great. They encamped upon the Janiculum Hill, and continued their retreat early the next morning. I came to Rome, met my old fellow Students, who were all happy to see me once more alive. The good Rector used me as he would his own son, and during my stay, insisted on my sleeping every night in the college, although this was a downright breach of their rules, and the porter waited every night till I thought proper to come to bed.– I was presented by General M'Donnell to King James, and to his second son then styled Duke of York, afterwards Cardinal, by the same title. The Genl. I had reason to believe spoke a great deal in my favour by the flattering reception I met with everywhere.

I left Rome once more in company with his Excellency, and rejoined our army at the town of Spoletto, where in a few days afterwards I saw a dreadful example of discipline. The enemy being pressed upon by us in their retreat, left a thousand men, all deserters from our army at different times, which they had formed into a Regiment, and put to guard a strong pass in their rear called Nocera, a town in the patrimony of St. Peter. I went with a strong detachment against Nocera, which we surrounded, attacked and took by assault two hundred of the

Chapter 4

garrison were killed in the assault, and 800 were made prisoners. In a few days afterwards two hundred of these deserters were shot, two hundred hanged and 400 sent to the gallies. I pitied one poor fellow, who in marching by knew me, said, then M'Donnell, you are still alive, don't you remember I was the last man alive with you when you got your third wound. I answered yes, I knew very well; "but how come you to be led to execution?' "O I was taken prisoner, and from severe usage was obliged to take part with the enemy, and being taken in arms, am now to be shot." I told him that I was very sorry for it, but could not now help him, it being forbidden to ask for the life of any of the condemned. About four minutes after, the poor fellow was shot among the rest.

The Austrian army got out of our reach, and marched by the Modenese in order to protect Lombardy, as another Spanish army and 12,000 French were forcing their way by the King of Sardinia's territories, to possess themselves of the above-mentioned country. We took our route by the Bolognese then struck across the Appenine Mountains to the Republic of Lucca. Had several smart actions on our march; sometimes forcing passes and at other times guarding our own rear, being necessitated to march by different routes and in different divisions, from the scarcity of provisions and ruggedness of the roads in these mountains. From Lucca we marched to Genoa, where we were joined by twelve hundred Genoese. About this time I lost my two most valuable friends and protectors, the excellent and valiant Lieut. Genl. M'Donnell, who had died of a fever occasioned by the fatigue of our last march, and his brother the Major Genl. within a few days after, of a fever also, occasioned by the festering of an old wound he had received in the shoulder, fifteen years before.

The Austrian army got before ours, by having taken an easier and shorter route, and got possession of a very strong pass, called the Buchetta about thirty or forty miles above Genoa, by which we must march to enter Lombardy on that

A Second Campaign

side. We attacked this pass and drove the enemy before us till we came to what is called the Key of Lombardy, Tortona, a very strong place, then garrisoned by five regiments. Upon the plains not far from this place all our different armies met to form a junction, viz. 20,000 Spaniards, 15,000 Neapolitans, 12,000 French, and 12,000 Genoese. We were drawn up in lines, and viewed by the Infant Don Philip, for whom we were to conquer the Duchies of Parma and Placentia.

The armies divided next day, that which I belonged to invested and laid seige to Tortona, which we took after four weeks of open trenches. The other grand division of the army went to the Milanese along with the Infant Don Philipe. After the reduction of Tortona the part of the army in which was, marched to Placenza, or Placentia, which surrendered without much trouble. Having to cross the river Po we made a floating Bridge of Mills (14) large Scows and Pontoons, between every two of them, in face of the enemy, by which our heavy

A French Street Vendor

Chapter 4

artillery was got to the Milan side of the Po. This was the last service which I helped to perform for the King of Spain. By dint of application and favour I obtained leave to go to France in order to join some troops intended by that power to assist Prince Charles Stuart then in Britain. My rank in the Spanish army at the time of getting leave of absence, was that of Lieutenant commanding and paying Colonel M'Donnell's company of the regiment Irlanda, and I had a promise of the first company that became vacant in the regiment ([15]).

Chapter 5

Return to Scotland

I set out for France accompanied by fourteen other Officers of our Irish regiments who had likewise got leave of absence to go to assist the Stuart cause in Britain. – At Genoa we hired a barge, and coasted all the way until we landed at Antibes in the south of France. Continued thence our route very happily for Paris. At the city of Lyons we met a number of French officers, who informed us that Charles Stuart had retreated from England, and had been attacked in Scotland at a place called Falkirk, fought there a battle in which the Highlanders had beat and chased the English cavalry and infantry of the field, very roughly handled. Continued our route for Paris in what is called the Diligence, this is a Coach which goes between Paris and Lyons, and is, next to riding post, reckoned the most expeditious and the cheapest mode of travelling in France.

Arrived at Paris where we remained about eight days. Here we held a consultation as to our future motions, when it was resolved by a majority that as Charles Edward had retreated from England, and the passage to Scotland was dangerous on account of the English Fleet, and also precarious on account of French politics, and as the spring was approaching, that they ought not to lose the ensuing campaign by their own fault, one and all except me, resolved to return to Italy. I observed to them that if Charles was triumphantly entering London, they would join him with great allacrity, that his affairs now seemed to require assistance, and that it was ungenerous not to give what aid we were capable of, to forward his interest, but I could not prevail on any of them to be of my opinion.

Chapter 5

French gentleman

I wrote to one Mr. Constable, then Secretary to the Duke of York, of the resolution of my comrades, and likewise of my own. By the return of the post I received orders from His Royal Highness to repair to Boulogne, which I immediately complied with. Upon knocking at Mr Constable's Chambre door, it was opened by the Duke, who chanced to be at the time with his Secretary. His Royal Highness welcomed me from Italy, and without allowing me to shift, introduced me to the Duke of Fitz James and to all the French General Officers and nobility then present. – General Lally colonel of a regiment of that name, and appointed Governor of Pondicherry, offered me a company and wished me to go along with him to Pondicherry, which I declined with proper acknowledgements. This gentleman after the reduction of Pondicherry by the British, was very unjustly beheaded in France.

Return to Scotland

I remained some weeks at Boulogne waiting the determination of the French Court; as a promise had been made to the Duke, which brought him from Italy, of being landed with a strong army in England, where the Stuart cause had many powerful adherents – but being disappointed of this succour he was obliged to send in single vessels what little aid could be procured; one of which sailed from Dunkirk with about 300 men and a number of Officers in the beginning of April, (1746). I was to have embarked in this vessel, but the Duke of York would not allow me, yet told me I should soon get leave to go. In a few days afterwards I was ordered to go to Dunkirk, where he soon arrived, and was next day asked to dinner by Marechal Clare, then commanding the French army in and about that place. Being considered to be one of the Duke's retinue, I was also asked to dinner. Lord Clare observing by my uniform that I did not belong to the troops about Dunkirk, enquired of the Duke what that youth was. The Duke told him it was a Highland gentleman of the name of M'Donell, a Lieut. in the Spanish army in Italy, upon which the Marechal addressing himself to me, said "Mr M'Donell I have a company now vacant in my regiment and it is this minute at your service." I rose from my seat, and with a modest blush thanked his Excellency for the honour he did me; said that I did not leave the service I was in, where I was beloved and esteemed, for any other reason than to risk my life in gratitude to my protectors and benefactors, the Stuart Royal family, to whom I owed every attachment besides. The Duke seemed very well pleased with my answer to the Marechal.

Two or three days after, the Duke left Dunkirk and went to Saint Omers; to which place I accompanied him. As we were going to part, he told me that I must take leave of him without any mark of distinction more than to a private gentleman, as he intended to travel incognito, so that we embraced and parted, he proceeding through Flanders, and I back to Dunkirk. Two days after my return, I was given to understand

Chapter 5

that the vessel intended for Scotland was ready to go to sea, this was a large Cutter, built in England, and was taken by the French when becalmed; she was the best sailor in Dunkirk. She was at this time a French privateer manned by fifty men. I Embarked at the Quay in company with twenty five more Officers, all Irish, going likewise to Scotland. I had scarcely got on board, when the Major of Clare's regiment standing of the Quay, (a great number of Irish Officers being there also) asked if one M'Donell was on board? I being the only one of that name there, answered, yes. Sir, said he, I have orders from His Royal Highness the Duke of York to let you have whatever sum of money you may please to call for. I returned for answer, that I already was under more obligations to His Royal Highness than I could ever repay; thanked the major, and said, that I had a sufficiency of money to bring me to my own country, and would get more there before it was spent, if I should deserve it.

We sailed the following night for Scotland, keeping a course well to the Northward. We were repeatedly chased, but none would come up with us. We intended to land at Inverness, and for that purpose lay-to at night in the Frith of Cromarty in order to land next morning. In the latter part of the night I was awakened by an ugly scream of one of the Officers, asked him what was the matter – he told me that he had dreamt the D—l had got hold of him by the small of the legs and was going to dash out his brains against the side of the Ship. I said to him that perhaps the D—l is not far off, went upon the deck and taking a view all round, observed a large Ship laying-to, between ours and the extrance of the Bay. I called the Captain of the Privateer; who, when he observed the Ship, ordered all sails to be set without any noise, so as to get clear before being seen, when that was affected we steered round by the Orkneys and made for Loch Broom. I got there the dismal news, that the battle of Culloden had been fought and lost the very day we sailed from Dunkirk, 16th

April, 1746, that many of my relations kindred and clansmen were killed; amongst the rest my uncle Scottos Donald M'Donell ([16]), and that the Highlanders were all dispersed, and no body knew what was become of the Prince Charles Edward.

Chapter 6

Skullduggery at Loch Broom

In consequence of this intelligence a council was held, in which it was resolved, that I being a native of the country, and one Capt. Lynch who left the Hungarian service to fight for the Stuart interest, should land, as I had letters from the Duke of York to his brother Prince Charles, and likewise the charge of 3000 pounds intended for the Prince's use, all the other officers were to return. I took only 1500L ashore with me, and the vessel sailed next morning back for France, with the rest of the Officers.

I sent for a gentleman styled Ardloch ([17]), of the name of M'Kenzie who had been a Captain in Prince Charles's army, who recommended me to another Capt. M'Kenzie commonly called Colin Dearg Laggy ([18]); hired a boat and crew to bring us to Laggy in little Loch Broom, where we found Old Colin Dearg, a Major of Cromarty's regiment, big William M'Kenzie of Killcoy ([19]), and Lieut. Murdoch M'Kenzie ([20]), of Cromarty's regiment with about 60 men, thought ourselves as safe as in the heart of France. Our baggage and little stores were carried by men to the house of Laggy. A fellow who carried my portmanteau told me it was d—d heavy. You cannot be surprised at that, I said, it being war time, and powder and ball necessary. Got to the house and were very well received by the forementioned officers by whom we understood that there were still some in arms of Prince Charles's men, viz., Glengarey's regiment who were my relations and kinsmen, and Cameron of Lochiel's, who was himself severely wounded in late action, and several other troops. With the help of the above Officers we engaged guides and a horse to carry our Portmanteaus, and being in the utmost haste to join the reported troops, begged for an early supper in order to set out in the beginning of the night.

My portmanteau was laid in the corner of the room in which we sat. Supper was served. It was dark, and no lights offered. Sat down to supper. The other officers, namely, Wm. M'Kenzie, of Kilcoy; Lieut. Murdoch M'Kenzie, and a gentleman of the name of Gordon, who was to be out of our company, sat to supper with us. Colin Dearg did not. The room we were in, was gradually filled with men, who stood behind us. I got up three or four times to look at my Portmanteau, saw it where I had placed it. Supper being over we took a single glass round of our stores, to Charles's health and better times, and being then told that the horse was ready, I started up, jumped to the corner for my Portmanteau to have it carried out, upon which the landlord told me, that he had got it put on the horse while we were drinking Charles's health. I suspected nothing of any harm, and set out on our journey. About half an hour after daylight we arrived at a gentleman's seat, Mr. M'Kenzie of Dundonald nephew to Colin Dearg ([21]),

I got up three or four times to look at my Portmanteau

Chapter 6

by whose recommendation we halted at the house. Mr. M'Kenzie was then at Inverness for fear of being suspected of favouring Charles's cause, but his lady was at home. Unloaded the horse, when Mr. Gordon complained that he could not accompany us farther as his shoes were worn out. I told him I would supply that deficiency by giving him a pair of mine which were in the upper covering of my Portmanteau. Then says he I must have them before we sleep. I told him to let us first take a nap. No, he returned, I will have them now, to try if they'll fit me. I went to the Portmanteau, unbuckled the upper straps and discovered a large cut, by which I immediately guessed some mischief had happened. Called Capt. Lynch, declared to him my suspicion; then before him and Mr. Gordon, examined the Portmanteau and found that a canvas bag containing 1000 guineas was gone. Lynch said, "it is your countrymen who have done this." "No reflections upon countries, Captain Lynch, returned I, there are more rogues in Ireland than in Scotland. Were we in France I'd pay you for your reflection; at present I do not choose to resent it. Let us go back to where this theft was committed; arm ourselves to the best advantage, and recover the money if possible."

This resolution being taken, I called the maid of the house, asked her if the lady was up. Was answered in the negative. Make her Capt. M'Donell's compliments and tell her I must instantly speak to her. She returned and told me I might use the freedom I asked. Upon which I went into the bedroom, the maid bearing me company. I told the lady the cause of my early visit – "that I was very happy for having made the discovery so early; for otherwise I would certainly have blamed her people for the theft, rather than suspect those under the denomination of officers and gentlemen but that now the case was quite plain. – Now Madam, here is a sack containing 500 guineas, which I give to you in charge; if I come back I will expect restitution – if killed, I bequeath it to your ladyship. God be with you, I wish you a good morning."

Skullduggery at Loch Broom

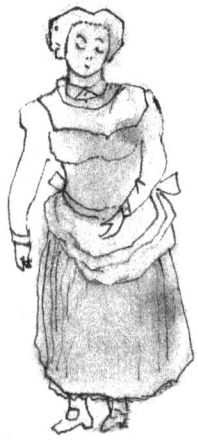

called a maid of the house

Captain Lynch and I with only one man to shew us the way, returned to Laggy. Sent in the man to tell the officers, and particularly Colin Dearg, to come out to speak to us. While the man was in, with our message, Captain Lynch told me that we had but to present our pistols to their breasts and kill two of them, if they would not instantly return us our money. This too peremptory demand I opposed, and told him I was of opinion, first to prove that Colin Dearg was himself the person who took the money, and not to pretend that we suspected in the least the others to be concerned in the theft – and to urge them to use their influence over him to induce him to return the stolen gold; and if it was true, that my people were still in arms, I would soon recover the money with a vengeance to the M'Kenzies; and further that my friends knew nothing yet of my return from abroad, and if we were killed, the perpetrators would obtain pardon by means of the letter I had from the Duke of York to his brother, and thus would go unpunished for taking our lives as well as the money. The three gentlemen

Chapter 6

came out followed by from twenty to thirty men. After a pretty cold salutation, I asked Colin Dearg for the gold taken out of my portmanteau at his house last evening. He answered that he knew nothing of the matter. "There" I returned, pointing to Capt. Lynch, "Is a man who saw the money put into the portmanteau." "Yes," says Lynch, "and can prove it was taken out at your house, and that it could not be taken out any where else." Colin Dearg said he would enquire about it of all the people about the house, and would return it if found, and so said the other gentlemen also. We allowed this mock work to go on, to see how it would end, expecting shame or remorse would work upon them to give it back, as if cut out and taken by some of their attendants. But when they reported that it could not be found, I opened upon Colin Dearg – told him plainly that he himself had taken it, and that if he did not immediately restore it to me, he would stand by the consequences, which might prove fatal to him. Upon this he re-entered his house, and the other two told us that we had better go and prosecute our journey, all their people standing armed by them. This I took for a word to the wise, and told Captain Lynch in French that we had best be gone, being too weak for the whole. As we withdrew we kept a sharp look out behind, resolved to shoot any that came armed within our reach from that quarter, but none presumed so far ([22]).

Chapter 7

The Truth Comes Out

Came to Lady Dundonald's – asked if she had any men near her home we could trust – she said that "she had some." We then asked her the favour of half a dozen armed men, which being procured, we placed two sentries and gave the command of the party to Mr. Gordon, with orders to alarm us instantly should any men be discovered approaching the house. The lady helped us to a plentiful breakfast, of which we had very great need. After that we took a good sleep (not less necessary) throwing ourselves on a bed dressed and armed as we were. The lady provided us with guides for our journey, upon whose fidelity she said we might depend, and who indeed behaved very well all along. Having made the lady a present of some bottles of choice French brandy, and of Mountain Malaga Wine, out of our travelling stock, with hearts full of gratitude we took a respectful leave of this most amiable lady and continued our journey for several days over wild and almost inaccessible mountains, being obliged to avoid all public roads for fear of falling in with any parties of English, as my comrade and I wore foreign uniforms.

After a very fatiguing march, we came to the side of Lochairkaig in Lochiel's country, where we met about 50 highland soldiers of my native part of the Country, commanded by my cousin Colonel Coll M'Donell younger of Barisdale, whose face I immediately recollected, and saluting him said I was glad to see him. He said that I had the advantage of him, that he had never seen me before. I then told him who I was; enquired about the rest of my relations; what number of men were yet in arms for Charles, and where they

Chapter 7

were? He told me that all was over – that Cameron of Lochiel was with 500 men at his seat of Achnacarrie; that Mr. Murray of Broughton one of Charles' Secretaries, and some officers were there likewise, and that he (Coll Borisdale) was going to raise more men; that most of Glengary's regiment would be there to-morrow under the command of Colonel Donald M'Donell of Largarry (Lochgarry), to try what terms could be obtained from the Duke of Cumberland, then at Fort Augustus, not many miles distant, where he advanced after defeating the Prince at Culloden. – That it was not known what was become of the Prince after the defeat, but that he was not killed in the battle. I told Borisdale that I would proceed to Achnacarrie to see Secretary Murray, and did not yet know what I should do after.

I went that same evening to Achnacarrie ([23]), and was most kindly received by Lochiel, tho' he was badly wounded, also by Secretary Murray, and the rest of Charles's party at that place – paid and dismissed our guides. After which Captain Lynch and I had a private interview with Mr. Murray, to whom I delivered the letters entrusted to my care by the Duke of York, and likewise the remaining 500 guineas for Charles's private use, supposing that the Secretary knew where he was to be found; (every circumspection being necessary, as a round sum of £30,000 sterling was offered for his head). I took Mr. Murray's receipt for the money and letters, and gave him an account in writing of the theft at Lochbroom ([24]). After this my comrade and I went to see an uncle and some cousins of mine who were heading some of my countrymen then at Achnacarrie. Took some refreshing rest, out of which we were awakened at break of day next morning by all the Highland Bagpipes playing the general, Cogga na si, having been alarmed by their scouts, who reported that the Duke of Cumberland had sent a much superior force by three different routes to surround them; the first division of which was already in sight at about a quarter of a mile distance. Our

The Truth Comes Out

whole force, when drawn out, did not exceed 800 men, who were ordered to march with all haste to the west end of Lochairkaig, which was executed just time enough to prevent our falling in with another division sent to obstruct our march by that route. After dusk we all separated – some went one way and some another. Captain Lynch and I went along with my friends to my native part of the Country – Knoidart.

I passed the greater part of the summer between Crowlin and Scottos, my father and grandfather's places of residence. Having got intelligence that a French Cutter had come to a place called Poolah (Poolewe) in the M'Kenzie Country, Captain Lynch thought proper to take a passage on board of her to France, which Country he reached in safety, and having entered the French service was the following year (1747) killed at the battle of Lafelt, or Vaal, in Flanders. By Captain Lynch I wrote to the Duke of York then in Italy, giving a full

provided us with guides for the journey

Chapter 7

account of all that befell me after my parting with his Royal Highness at St. Omers, till Captain Lynch parted with me in the Highlands.

I had put on a resolution never to leave Scotland while Charles was in the country. I had almost every day reports of his being so hemmed in by his pursuers that is was impossible for him to escape being either killed or taken, so close was he pursued. But to the eternal honour of my Countrymen, they despised the alluring reward of £30,000 sterling offered for his head, and though overcome in battle by superior numbers, were above bribery – screened him from his inveterate enemies, till such time as two stout Privateers from St. Maloes in France, came to Lochnannough (Lochnanuagh) in Arisoig on the west coast of Invernesshire, where he embarked and landed safely in France, after going through many more difficulties and dangers than ever his predecessor Charles II had experienced.

Some time before the Prince was made acquainted with the arrival of the above ships, I had, in company with some of my friends embarked with my little baggage to take a passage for France in order to rejoin the Spanish army; but the Prince not appearing at the time expected, he being concealed at a great distance from the place, I was prevailed on by the entreaties of my nearest relations to return home with them. The only motive that proved decisive against my resolution of going abroad was my father's sickness, he being then in so violent a consumption that it must soon put a period to his life, leaving a numerous and weak family of children, of which I was the oldest unprovided for, and my grandfather, Aeneas of Scottos, being old and infirm. I thought it a duty incumbent to attend to the call of nature which pleaded strongly in favor of the distressed children, and wave the sure prospect I had of advancing myself both to riches and honor ([25]). My father tho' upon his death bed, rather regretted than rejoiced at my return. He paid the debt of nature soon after, like a true christian, with

The Truth Comes Out

all his senses about him – left my mother and the rest of my family to my charge, and I took all the care of them in my power.

The following winter I took a jaunt to the M'Kenzie's Country accompanied only by a single servant, to discover if I could, how the 1000 guineas cut out of my portmanteau at Lochbroom had been disposed of. Lodged a night with a Mr. M'Kenzie of Torridon ([26]), who had been a Lieutenant Colonel in my cousin Coll Borisdale's Regiment in Prince Charles's service. Early next morning while the lady of the house was ordering breakfast, I went to take a solitary turn and met a well dressed man in highland cloaths also taking the morning air. After civil salutations to each other, I entered into discourse with him about former transactions in that Country. He of himself began to tell me about French officers that came to Lochbroom – how the 1000 guineas had been cut out of one of their portmaneaus by Colin Dearg, Major Wm. M'Kenzie of Kilcoy, and Lieutenant Murdoch M'Kenzie from Dingwall – all officers of Lord Cromartie's Regiment, being all equally concerned; and how not only those who acted the scene, but all the people in that part of the country had been despised and ridiculed for their mean and dastardly behaviour; but that had his (M'Kenzie who was speaking to me) advice been taken, there should never have been a word about the matter. The following dialogue then ensued. Question: "And pray Sir what did you advise?" Answer: "To cut off both their heads, a very sure way indeed!" Q: "What were they, or of what Country?" A: "The oldest and a stout like man, was Irish. The youngest and very strong like, was a M'Donell of the family of Glengarry." Q: "How was the money divided?" A: "Colin Dearg got 300 guineas, William Kilcoy got 300 guineas, and Lieutenant Murdoch M'Kenzie got 300 guineas." Q: "What became of the other hundred?" A: "Two men who stood behind the Irish Captain with drawn dirks ready to kill him, had he observed Colin Dearg cutting open the portmanteau,

Chapter 7

got 25 guineas each; and I and another man prepared in like manner for the young Captain M'Donell, got 25 guineas each." Q: "You tell the truth, you are sure." A: "As I shall answer I do." Q: "Do you know to whom you are speaking?" A: "To a friend and one of my own name." "No, you d—d rascal," seizing him suddenly by the breast with my left hand, at the same instant twitching out my dirk with the right, and throwing him upon his back, "I am that very M'Donell." I own I was within an ace of running him through the heart, but some sudden reflection struck me – my being alone, and in a place where I was in a manner a stranger, among people which I had reason to distrust, I left the fellow upon his back, and re-entered the house in some hurry. My landlord Mr. M'Kenzie of Torridon met me in the entry, asked where I had been. I answered "taking a turn." "Have you met anything to vex you?" "No" I returned smiling. "Sir" says he, "I ask pardon, you went out with an innocent and harmless countenance, and you come in with a fierceness in your aspect past all description." Mr M'Kenzie, said I, "none of your scrutinizing remarks, let us have our morning!" "With all my heart," he replied. Soon after, being a little composed, I related to him my morning adventure. He remarked that the man was a stranger to him, and had been a soldier in Lord Cromartie's Regiment. That very day I quitted that part of the country and returned home, where I continued some time.

Chapter 8

"Ill Got, Ill Gone!"

John M'Donell of Glengary, my cousin, whose Castle, by the Duke of Cumberland's positive orders, was burnt, the foundation undermined and blown up, to prevent the possibility of its being repaired in future, and who was himself sent a prisoner to Edinburgh Castle, on suspicion of attachment to Charles, but for want of evidence against him, was set at liberty, was my Chief ([27]). I went to Invergary to pay my respects to him, and in course of the visit I informed him of my usage by the M'Kenzies, and in what manner they had divided the plunder among them. Told him, I wanted to make one more effort by means of Mr. M'Kenzie of Dundonald, Colin Dearg's nephew, a man of influence in that part of the country, and a man of honour to recover, if not the whole, at least some part of what had been stolen. But as no armed force could be put together to recover the money that he would please order four or five of the bravest and strongest of his men to accompany me by way of life guard, least the M'Kenzies should take it into their heads to murder me, if they found me unprepared for resistance. The Chief readily granted my request. Myself and five men were as well appointed with arms and resolution as I could desire. We went on our journey, they without fear, and I in no expectation of being recognized by any person in that part of the country called Lochbroom; as upon my first landing there I was in full regimentals, with a wig and black bag, a la mode de Paris, but now in a highland dress with a blue bonnet and my own short hair, so that whatever place we came to, I was supposed to be some attainted gentleman of note belonging to Prince Charles who

Chapter 8

had not as yet an opportunity of escaping out of the Kingdom. We came to Dundonald's, to whom I told in confidence who I was, and the cause of my visit. He told me that he would send to his uncle, to meet him in a certain place, but that if he knew of my being there, he would not appear. By what means he found out my being in that part of the country I never learned, but he came to the house appointed, accompanied by 40 or 50 men, where his nephew and I with my five followers were before him. Having observed Colin Dearg's men all armed with short sticks shaped like axe handles in their hands, and dirks under their great coats, I told my men aside, that in all probability the opposite party were resolved to give some very serious insult. The house of meeting was all one floor without partitions, and the door in the middle. I told my men to sit near the door within, and to take special care that none should sit between any two of them, and to be sure to keep the command of their arms, that as for me I would seat myself between the uncle and nephew, and it being then night, if any serious offensive motion was made by the opposite party, that without further order or minding me, they must take possession of the outside of the door; and two of them, which I named, to defend the door with their broadswords that none should get out alive of those within. The other three to set both ends of the house on fire, that all within might perish; and told them further, that I was determined to kill the uncle and nephew at once, one with my pistol and the other with my dirk, to knock out the light, and stab every one that came in my way. That if I chanced to come alive to the door they would know my voice, and if not, to let all within perish along with me. I had a good chance of escaping, as they would kill one another thro' mistake in the dark. This being concerted, I went boldly in and seated myself where I proposed – my men did the same.

After a short pause, Dundonald mentioned the cause of our present meeting in as becoming a manner as the subject would admit of; to which an evasive answer was returned by his

"Ill Got, Ill Gone!"

*A well dressed man in Highland Cloaths
taking the morning air*

uncle, Colin Dearg, pretending to deny the fact. I then took him up, and proved that he himself was the very man who, with his own hands had taken the gold out of my portmanteau after cutting it open with some sharp instrument. This I said openly in the hearing of all present. To which I got no other reply than that "the money was gone, and could not be accounted for." I returned that "If the cash was squandered, the reward due to such action was yet extant" – and being asked what that was, I answered, "the gallows." At this expression the whole got up standing, and seeing them all looking towards me, I drew my dirk and side pistol, and

Chapter 8

presenting one to my right and the other to my left, swore that if any motion was made against my life, I would dispatch Dundonald and his uncle, who seeing me ready to put threat in execution, begged of their people for the love of God, to be quiet, which was directly obeyed. In the mean time my men had taken immediate possession of the outside of the door, and were prepared to act according to my orders. I called to them to stay where they were, but none of the people in the house knew what they went out for. Dundonald assured me that all the money had been wasted without any visible benefit to the thieves; which put me in mind of the old saying "ill got ill gone."

Dundonald and I returned that same night to his house, and next morning I began my march for home without any further satisfaction – but had I had twenty men equal to the five that accompanied me, I would, in spite of the whole name of M'Kenzie then present, have forced away Colin Dearg and got him hanged on the first tree I could meet with. Nothing worth mentioning occurred on my way back. I arrived at Glengarry – after waiting on the Chief, dismissed my attendants with suitable acknowledgements. I then made for my own place, where I remained improving my little property, and amusing myself in all the parties that that part of the Country with a numerous society of gentlemen, well polished and educated, could afford. Next year I got certain intelligence that Colin Dearg died as poor as a beggar, and that big William Kilcoy, the Major (formerly made such honourable mention of) in coming down the stair of his own house to take horse to bring home a lady he had lately married ([28]), got a fall and dislocated his neck; so that the thieves were punished without my concurrence, which God forgive me, I was not sorry for.

Chapter 9

Captured

Doctor M'Donell of Kylles, my relation ([29]), an eminent Physician being on a visit to me, insisted on my going in the evening with him to fish at a Rock at the entrance of Lochcarron, opposite to my house, and about a mile distant.

Doctor McDonell of Kylles, an eminent physician

Chapter 9

We fished for some time and had good sport. A vessel hove in sight making for the sound of the Isle of Skye – it falling calm, the Doctor pressed me to go with him on board the vessel, to see if he could get some articles he wanted to purchase for house use. I told him I would willingly go, but being in dishabille did not like to go anywhere, but told him that if there should be strangers that he must pass me off for his ploughman, who could not speak a word of English. Pulled towards the ship the size of which we could not properly discern, it being in the dusk of the evening. Upon our approach we were hailed and ordered to come on board, and getting alongside to avoid giving any umbrage or shewing distrust, the boats' crew and all of us went on board. The ship proved to be the Porcupine sloop of war, commanded by Captain John Ferguson ([30]), and mounting sixteen carriage guns. The Doctor saluted the officers on deck and was brought by the sailing master down to his cabin. In a careless manner walked forward and backward upon the quarter deck, observed the Captain walking alone, who after eyeing me three or four times, came and went past and round me different times, then went to his cabin. I went to call the Doctor in order to depart, the master and he were drinking cheerfully together, to which he was rather partial; got a glass of grog, and the Doctor said he would be with me in a trice. I retired with an awkward bow. Upon my second application for departing, the Doctor who had got into his cups, said to the sailing master in my hearing by the great oath, "that is as good a gentleman as I am." After getting upon deck, the Doctor was told that we could not be allowed to depart before next day. We were consequently detained, boats' crew and all for the night.

The Porcupine sloop of war was stationed on the west coast to cruize and get information, to apprehend outlawed persons, and to burn and destroy the houses and effects of such as had been in arms against the government ([31]), and also to transport troops to and from the mainland to the Islands. Captain

Captured

Ferguson went early next morning to see and get what intelligence he could from Captain Allan M'Donald of Knock (³²), in Slate, a part of the Isle of Skye, who was the greatest spy and informer in all Scotland, and by all accounts the greatest coward. Captain Ferguson told him that he believed he had last night taken young Borisdale cloathed in a manner to disguise him – but that he (Ferguson) knew by the first step he walked upon deck that he was a gentleman in disguise, tho' pretending not to understand a word of English, and that he answered exactly the description that he had of the person of the attainted young Borisdale. The Captain of the spies enquired minutely of Ferguson about the shape, size, colour of hair and eyes of the person detained, all which answered; and asked further whether he had any marks of sores or wounds about the neck, and was told he had. The spy Captain then said it was not Borisdale, but a greater rebel, who kept up a constant correspondence with the enemies of his Country, who was in every respect a very great rogue, and not to let him go, or even be admitted to bail, as he could by many evidences prove him guilty of different acts of high treason.

Capt. Ferguson on his return called for me upon deck, and clapping his hand upon my shoulder said, "you are my prisoner." I asked by what authority he presumed to take me. "Oh, ho! he replied, you speak English I find." I answered, "more than you Captain Ferguson would wish, and other languages if I please; but do not imagine that you can frighten me, I have before now looked in the face of as great men as you, and you may rest assured that your action in apprehending me without any authority but your own arbitrary will, shall be examined into. He then said "by G—d you shall see London." I answered I am very glad of it, that I had already seen the greatest Cities in many parts of Europe, and that a sight of London would afford me infinite pleasure, and added that I hoped he would pay for my passage to that City, and for my way back again; in short I nettled him as much as I

Chapter 9

could. The Doctor and my boats' crew were set at liberty, and I alone detained. Bail to the amount of two thousand pounds was offered for my appearance before the Justiciary Court in Great Britain, but no bail could be taken as I was accused of different acts of high treason.

Chapter 10

Fort William

I continued on board a prisoner, for four weeks, guarded night and day by a sentry, till we came to the Sound of Mull, where lay a 20 gun ship commanded by Captain Gardner, Commodore of the West Coast ([33]). Captain Ferguson went on board the Commodore and made a report of his prisoner, and I was ordered on board his ship in the evening. I heard the sailors who were mostly Irish, say one to another. "There is some one to be put in irons tonight," but did not imagine that it was I. About night-fall a midshipman with a party secured my feet with a heavy iron bolt. I asked the midshipman whose name was Maitland ([34]), from Edinburgh, what was the reason for my being so unworthily treated? He said the he was very sorry to see me used in such a manner, but that he could not tell the cause, and that he dare not disobey his Captain's orders. With downright vexation, I was in raging fever all night, and would have blown up the ship and all hands if it lay in my power. After passing the most mortifying night of my life, the same midshipman came next morning to unbolt me. I

Chapter 10

asked him if he would have the goodness to tell the Captain that the prisoner wished to speak to him; he said he would with the greatest of pleasure. I was consequently ordered to the cabin, attended by a guard, who remained at the cabin door when I entered. I told Captain Gardner that I was surprised at the unworthy manner in which I was used on board his ship and by his orders, particularly as he had the character of a worthy and humane man; hoped that he would not take it amiss if I enquired the cause of his particular resentment against me, as I was ignorant of giving any cause of being used in such a barbarous and horrid manner. That I had been among cruel enemies, but that his treatment of me was above all the barbarity I had ever experienced, and that even Captain Ferguson, though worse than any man I ever knew, did not offer me such indignity. I stood during this address; Captain Gardner bid me sit down, and placing himself by my side, said that the reason of the treatment I underwent by his orders, was, that my own countryman, Captain Ferguson, made him believe that if I was not properly secured I would some how destroy the ship, or in spite of them all swim ashore. I replied that it was incredible to a man possessed of less good sense than him, that any man could in any way accomplish such feats in defiance of the ship's crew, that as to swimming it was an exercise I never practiced – that he was however pleased to order good sinkers to prevent my attempting it. Upon this he got up and taking a sheet of paper from a locker or cupboard and putting it into my hands, said that he need not ask if I could read. It was an accusation full of various crimes, the least of which, if true, would have condemned any man. I read the whole to the end and smiled. "What!" says he, "do you laugh at it, it would hang twenty men?" "Yes Sir, I do laugh at it, for there is not a word of truth from beginning to the end of it." He said that he should be very glad of that on my account, and moreover, as he had used me ill, he would in future make what amends he could; that his station prevented his acting according to his inclination, otherwise that I should be of his mess; that, however, I should mess with his officers to whom he would take care to recommend me. The same evening, orders came from Edinburgh, to send me without loss of time to Fort William, being the nearest fortress, and in the District to which I belonged.

Early next morning the ship's pinnace was made ready, and the ship's Lieutenant, Mr. Donaldson, six midshipmen, and from sixteen to eighteen sailors, and a coxswain, all armed, were ordered to land me at Fort William. I took leave of Captain Gardner in a friendly manner, and after an agreeable passage of some hours got to Fort William. The sailors who were Irish, told me by the way, in their language, that if I was afraid of my life, when I came to land, to run away; that they would fire, but would take care not to touch me. I thanked them, and told them there was no danger of me. I was delivered in proper form on the beach, by the escorting party of seafaring men to a party of land forces. Young Mr. Maitland the midshipman, who seemed the most sensibly touched with my situation, at parting told me in French, that I was indebted to Captain Allan M'Donald of Knock, in the Isle Skye, for all my sufferings. I replied in the same language, that I knew that to be the case.

I was locked up in a room in the Fort, and was not a little surprised to find my cousin Alexander M'Donell ([35]), second son of Coll Borisdale, a prisoner in the same room, and was well pleased to have a companion. Two soldiers with fixed bayonets were placed at the door to watch us. We had the liberty when we thought proper to walk upon the ramparts to take the air, always attended by the two armed soldiers. My companion to whom confinement was new, and warlike apparatus strange, looked and gazed at every thing that struck his fancy, examining and peeping thro' the embrazures. I told him that he was acting very wrong in seeming to examine any thing; that by his ill timed curiosity we should certainly lose

Chapter 10

the great advantage allowed us of going upon the ramparts, and that on the least information, the Governor would interpret his conduct in a wrong sense. Next day informing the sergeant of the guard that we wanted to take an airing on the ramparts as usual, he told us that it was forbidden by the Governor, and that all the ladders about the Fort were given in charge of the guard. I looked at my friend, observed to him that I expected what happened, but that now there was no remedy, we must bear our misfortune patiently. In a few days after he was set at liberty, having only been accused of some rash expressions against Mungo Campbell ([36]), the Factor appointed by the Crown, upon his father Coll Borisdale's estate.

During the short time that Alexander M'Donell was with me in the prison at Fort William, his eldest brother Archibald Borisdale ([37]), for whom I was first arrested; John M'Donald Esqr. of Morar, and black Ronald ([38]) a natural son of Archibald Borisdale, father of Coll, and my grand uncle, were made prisoners by means of Allan M'Donald of Knock, (Captain of the guides and spies,) formerly mentioned. Allan Knock had received a complete drubbing from black Ronald, at which Archibald Borisdale Junior, and John M'Donald Morar, married to Mary M'Donell, daughter of Coll Borisdale, chanced to be present. These gentlemen passed by Fort William, in custody, on their way to Edinburgh. Thus, this Captain Allan revenged his private quarrels under cover of his attachment to government, and got these gentlemen sent under a strong guard to Edinburgh Castle.

Altho' I was glad of young Alexander M'Donell Borisdale's enlargement, I felt myself at his departure very lonesome for want of company. Shortly afterwards, however, a gentleman from the Isle of Skye, Rory M'Donald of Fortymenruck or Camiscross ([39]), was introduced into my prison room. This was a gentleman with whom I was always very intimate, and a near neighbour to where I lived, whose vivacity would cheer any man's spirits. He was in the same manner with black Ronald taken by the Captain of the guides and spies, for having given him the said Captain a consummate beating as a reward for some impertinent language he made use of towards this Rory M'Donald. He was maliciously accused of having tortured a woman so that she died of the effects of the torture, which was afterwards found to be a falsehood.

Chapter 11

Allan Knock

I think it now high time to relate the cause of this spite and malice of Allan Knock against me, which I will relate without alteration or aggravation, and as far as I remember it was as follows. In one of my jaunts of pleasure to visit my relations and acquaintances in the Isle of Skye, I lodged the first night as usual after leaving home with Rory M'Donald now my fellow prisoner, and taking my departure early next day, for that part of Lord M'Donalds's estate called Troternish, came in the evening to Portree, or Port Royal, so called because King James V of Scotland landed there, when on a tour through the Western Islands of the Kingdom. I went into a tavern to take some refreshment after a march of twenty miles, being the days' journey; desired the landlord to get me something to drink. Upon which he informed me that there were some gentlemen in the next room who he was sure would like to have the pleasure of my company, if I thought proper to indulge them. I enquired of him who they were, he told me their names. Went out and returned instantly with an invitation from them for me. I joined them – some I knew, others I had seen before; took a share of what they had, then I called for more. One of the company, Mr Nicholson of Scorbreck, head of a tribe of that name, whose self and predecessors were vassals and landholders on Lord M'Donald's estate from time immemorial, said that he did not choose to drink any more, and upon my asking his reason, said that he was sometimes when warmed with liquor subject to blunder out something that might give offence to strangers. I observed to him that if it a was natural failing, that for my own part I would not mind it, but to take care to retract his words immediately if provoking. Upon beginning with what I had called for, I proposed the health of Rory M'Donald my last nights landlord, which passed round. Mr. Nicholson asked me why I did not propose the health of my cousin Allan M'Donald, Knock. I told him in reply that Allan laid under very bad imputations. And pray, Sir, said he, what are they? I answered that I knew them only from hearsay. And what did you hear? I have heard that he is a coward, an informer, and of course a scoundrel, whose health any gentleman would scorn to drink. And, said he, do you really believe him a coward? I answered that it was his general character. Then, said he, will you send him a challenge, and if he does not answer it I will? Sir, I replied, I have my sword by me, and you have yours – what should time be lost for? So turn out this instant, and if you can you shall have what you want. He got up, sneaked out of the company, got away I knew not how or where to – but I never saw him since. He certainly however, reported to his nephew Allan M'Donald, Knock, my having called him a coward in public company. Nicholson was uncle to Allan Knock, being brother to his mother.

Chapter 12

Freedom

My fellow prisoner, Rory M'Donald and I passed our time merrily tho' prisoners, and were continually visited by the gentlemen of most note in the neighbourhood. – Viz., the Camerons, Stuarts of Apin, and a number of our own clan, who came, not like the comforters of Holy Job; but with a real spirit of friendship to alleviate our distress and to pass some time with us in mirth and jollity. In the meantime neither of us

to pass some time in mirth and jollity

were idle in endeavouring to obtain our liberation. I in particular, pestered my lawyer at Edinburgh, Roderick M'Leod, Writer to the Signet (⁴⁰), always by letters blaming him for neglect, altho' I very well knew that he was using every means in his power to bring my affairs to a speedy conclusion, which he at last in part effected. Orders were sent from the Admiralty to Captain Ferguson, then laying at Greenock, to send what evidence he had against me to Fort William. He took care however, first to examine all those he was to send, and finding that they could evidence nothing of any consequence, sent a letter by one of his midshipmen, to Mr. Douglass (⁴¹), then undersheriff of the County, and residing at Fort William, an ignorant, weak, and poor wretch, purporting that altho' nothing should appear to my detriment by the evidences, that he was under the necessity of sending in obedience to the orders of his superiors – that notwithstanding, he must not admit me to bail, nor discharge me until he should know what Allan M'Donald (the Captain of the guides and spies) had to accuse me of.

This rascal, (Knock) was then at London on behalf of government, receiving the reward of his prosecution of better men than himself; and as already stated, availed himself of the authority of government, and under pretences of zeal in the Royal cause in these troublesome times – to avenge private grudges. Upon my informing my lawyer of a second commitment, Knock was compelled to send a list of his evidences, which he did, amounting to sixteen in number, all gentlemen of the first rank and respectability, in the Isle of Skye, who were ordered to be sworn by Mr. M'Leod of Ulnish, Sheriff deput of that District (⁴²). This gentleman being both my friend and relation, as well as the friend of justice, protracted the time as much as he could, for fear that anything should turn out to my disadvantage, by examining the gentleman separately at their own houses. By this friendship of his, it is true, I was kept longer in prison than I should have

Chapter 12

been; for I could not obtain my liberty until such time as every individual evidence had been taken and reported.

Of all this numerous list of evidences, there was only one that gave any thing that could in the least affect me. One gentleman mentioned that to the best of his recollection he saw my great coat open in jumping over a dyke, and that he thought he observed me have a philibeg and a hanger at my side. This part of the evidence, my friend the Sheriff kept to himself, and forwarded the others. So that all these treasons and other crimes alleged against me by the Captain of the guides and spies, turned out to be malicious calumnies and lies, the last spiteful resource of baseness and cowardice. After a confinement of three quarters of a year for imaginary crimes, I was at long last set at liberty. At the time of being taken up, I had my mother, and a throng family of minor brothers and sisters to support by my industry, who suffered considerably from my long confinement, and the total neglect of my affairs.

Douglas, the under Sheriff, by whose commitment I was detained, on credit of Captain Ferguson's letter, I intended to prosecute for false imprisonment. But the poor d—l had no means, and it would be only throwing away good money without any prospect of recovering. I was therefore forced to make myself easy. He soon after lost his place. Captain Ferguson, the first cause of my trouble was always at a great distance from me, and generally at sea. The Captain of the guides and spies was secured by the law, as he had only acted for the Crown by impeaching me of high treason. So that all the revenge I was able to take of him was that after his return from London, where he had been doing some good offices for his friends, and impeaching those he did not think such, and getting the reward of his villainies in ready cash, I met him at Glenelg in a mixt and public company; asked what I had done to offend him, and why he prosecuted me in such a spiteful manner? "I" said he, "I was always very fond of you as my relation, and would be very sorry to do you any harm." "You lie, you scoundrel." I returned, "and I believe I know the cause of your unmanly spite. I called you a coward at Portree by the report of other, and your cowardly uncle who promised to resent the expression and ran away with fear has without doubt informed you of it. I have already suffered for that expression, and now I repeat in the presence of all those gentlemen, that you are an arrant coward and a scoundrel." He immediately left the company, and put himself under the protection of the garrison at Glenelg, and afterwards never

and lived a most happy life upon my property

Chapter 12

went from there without being attended by a couple of armed soldiers. I have since been told that he was sorry for what he had done towards me – was afraid that I would spend my all, then kill him and afterwards make my escape to some foreign country.

In the foregoing sheets you have all that I can at this time remember of the early and most active part of my life. The few following lines will inform you in short words of what followed. I was in love with your mother([43]) at the time I had the misfortune of being taken up for young Borisdale. Some time after my enlargement from prison, for fear of some unlucky accident taking place which might prevent our union, notwithstanding our mutual attachment, we got married and lived a most happy life for a number of years upon my property. At last my disposition given rather to roving, induced me to leave my native soil, and come to this great Continent of America, where I have resided ever since.

Notes

(1) Third son of Charles Innes of Drumnagask and nephew of Father Thomas Innes the historian. He became principal of the Scots College in Paris in 1738 and died in 1752. (Dr Grub's Preface to 'The Civil and Ecclesiastical History of Scotland', p.xxiii. Spalding Club, 1853.)

Mr Lang erroneously calls him "brother of Thomas Innes."

(2) Avignon remained in the possession of the Popes till 1791.

(3) The Franciscan Observants were called *Cordelieres* in France because of a cord worn round the waist.

(4) This war arose out of the troubles that followed the death of the Emperor Charles VI, and the succession of his daughter Maria Theresa. Charles of Bourbon, son of Philip V, of Spain, had become King of Naples. Philip claimed certain Italian territory, and the Neapolitan army was placed at his disposal. The whole facts, including the story of the campaigns, described in Colonel Macdonald's narrative, are given in Colletta's 'History of Naples,' translated by F.S. Horner, Edinburgh, 1858.

(5) [This gentleman was born in Ireland and had left it and joined this brigade, as many of his countrymen did about this time.]

(6) For a full account of this capitulation, see Todhunter's 'Life of Sarsfield.' It is well known how grossly the fundamental provisions of the Treaty of Limerick were violated by William of Orange and his English parliament. Referring to the expatriation of Sarsfield's army, Mr Todhunter observes (p. 196): "Thus began that flight of the 'Wild Geese' which went on through the reigns of Anne and the first Georges, filling the ranks of the armies of Europe with

the flower of the youth of Ireland. It cost England dear in more ways than one, and caused an English King to curse the unjust laws which deprived him of such soldiers."

(7) These were Angus Macdonald of Scotus, Alastair Dubh of Glengarry, John of Sandaig and Archibald of Barrisdale, all sons of Ranald, who became chief of Glengarry in 1680 on the death of Angus, Lord Macdonell and Aros.

(8) The Austrian General Braun.

(9) For the death of Colonel Donald Macdonnel, see Colletta, *supra*, i. p. 178.

(10) [Hunts foot—i.e., leg of a dog, a term of reproach with the Germans.]

(11) [Previous to this a Croat, taking my gold-laced hat and putting it upon his own head, coolly asked me how he looked in it. He then with his sabre cut off my que and took it along with him.]

(12) [The Austrians attacked and entered Viletri with such vigour that the King of Naples had not time to draw on his boots till he got out of town. A Spanish General Officer was surprised and made prisoner in his quarters while at breakfast by an Austrian officer of high rank, who, at the other's invitation, sat down along with his prisoner to breakfast, during which the Spanish officer got up to the window, observed the Austrians retire, driven out by the Spanish forces. He turns to his guest and said to him, 'You are now my prisoner, for your troops are driven out, and ours have again possession of the town.' They sat down again to finish their breakfast. Much severe fighting took place in the streets; all the windows were broke by the balls. Such was the number killed that to clear a passage the bodies were in the evening thrown in heaps on each side the streets.]

(13) [A captain of artillery came one day to the hospital to have a boil, which he had in a very awkward part, dressed. Everyone was inquiring of him what action he had been wounded in. He was directed to lay on his face. A surgeon

began to examine and feel the boil, not over tenderly, when the captain, who had his boots on, struck him violently on the side of the face with both heels and knocked him over. This scene set all our wounds (about 200 officers) a-bleeding with the force of laughter, and the surgeons had to dress them all anew.]

(14) [On the River Po there are floating mills built on large scows that go up and down the river to grind pain.]

(15) [On leaving his regiment to join the prince, Spanish John received the following certificate from his colonel:–

"Nous Colonel du Regiment d'Infanterie d'Irlande, de St Jacques, certifions que le Sieur Jean Macdonell de Glengary, sous Lieutenant au dit Regiment s'est toujours comporte pendant tout le temps qu'il y a servi en Gentilhomme d'honneur brave Officier, et avec une conduite irreprochable a tout egard; en foy de quoy nous lui avons donne le present. Fait a Plaisance le douzieme Janvier, mil sept cent quarante six."

"Macdonell."]

(16) Donald M 'Donell, younger of Scottos, was a handsome and well-bred man, romantically brave and highly esteemed by Prince Charles Edward. Many anecdotes are related of his intrepidity and humanity. The morning of the battle of Culloden, a French officer, after viewing the position of both armies, remarked to Scottos that, from the bad position of Charles's army and fewness of their numbers, they must inevitably be defeated, to which Scottos replied that they had only to act as they were ordered. He was of that part of the Highlanders that charged the English line, and when Charles's forces gave way he was led off the field wounded by two of his men. Finding the pursuit coming too close, he desired the men to leave him, as his wound was mortal, and save themselves by flight. Gave them his watch, dirk, purse, &c., to bring home to his wife, and desired them to turn his face to the enemy, that they might not think he was running away. After getting away some distance the men looked behind them and

saw the dragoons despatch him.] In 'Clan Donald,' vol. iii. 324, reference is made to a curious story of the effect that he was only wounded, and with others was carried off by marauders who had landed from a ship at night, and sold into slavery, ending his days in the hands of Turkish pirates.

(17) John Mackenzie of Ardloch. He married Sibella, daughter of Kenneth Mackenzie I. of Dundonnell.

(18) Dearg = red. Also called Colin Roy, see note 22. In Mackenzie's 'History of the Mackenzies,' p.283, he is called Colin Riabhach, and said to have married a daughter of Simon Mackenzie, Loggie.

(19) Major William Mackenzie, brother of Colin Mackenzie of Kilcoy, in the Black Isle.

(20) Lieutenant Murdoch Mackenzie, son of Bailie Colin Mackenzie of Dingwall. (List of persons concerned in the Rebellion of 1745, Scot. Hist. Soc., 1st Series, vol. viii., p.78.)

(21) Kenneth, son of Kenneth Mackenzie II. of Dundonnell. He married in 1737 Jean, daughter of Sir Kenneth Mackenzie of Scatwell.

(22) A curious sequel to the robbery is recorded in a letter dated Dingwall, 10th March 1747:–

"Saturday last Alex. Mackenzie of Lentron and John Mackenzie of Torridon two rebel officers of Lord Cromarties regt. came to the place with a party of men to the number of 16 or 17 armed with guns swords and pistols and forcibly carried away Murdoch Mackenzie another of the officers of Lord Cromarties regt. . . . It is said that the reason for apprehending Murdoch is that he might deliver up to these gentlemen officers some money which he had in his custody that was landed in Corgach a Port on Lord Cromarty's estate in the Highlands. This ship came to the Highlands sometime after the Battle of Culloden and delivered to Major William Mackenzie brother to the Laird of Culoy [Kilcoy] and to Colin Mackenzie alias Roy [or Dearg] brother to Dundonald and to the above Murdoch

Notes

Mackenzie a portmanteau containing £3000 and upwards. The king's troops being then in the country the 3 officers divided the money for their own private use. But it is now given out that there's an order from the Pretender requiring these gentlemen to deliver up the money to the gentlemen who still adhere to his interest in this country to subsist themselves and their adherents who are still so audacious as to keep together a small body of armed men and do openly frequent their own houses and other publick places." ('More Culloden Papers' vol.p. 158.)

(23) "A small number of Locheils people arrived in the evening with an account that the rest were on their march under Dungallon and some hours afterwards a Spanish and French officer who had landed some days before in Loch Cruen [? Broom] from on board a ship in which there were a number of officers who upon hearing the melancholy situation that things were thereon returned to France – but these two gentlemen continued their rout on account of a large pacquet of Letters they were discharged with, containing despatches for the P—ce the Marquis de Guille and others." (Murray of Broughton's Memorials.' p.282. Scot. Hist. Soc., 1st Series, vol. xxvii.

(24) In an appendix to Chambers's 'History of the Rebellion' is printed (pp. 515 et seq) an account of charge and discharge by Murray of Broughton, transcribed, as Bishop Forbes states, from a document in Murray's own handwriting. It contains the following entry:–

"From a French officer who landed on the east (sic) coast with   2000 guineas   £1000

"Note.– This French officer was charged with 2000 guineas, but said he had 1000 taken from him as he passed thro' the Mackenzies country and gave in an account of deductions from the other 1000. But as Mr Murray can not charge his memory with the extent of the sum he has charged himself with one thousand pounds tho' he still thinks he did not receive quite so much."

Notes

(25) [The famous Conde de O'Reilly, who was for a long time at the head of the Spanish army, was a subaltern at the same time with Colonel M'Donell in the Irish Brigade in the Spanish service. They had fought side by side in Italy in 1745-6, and were upon the most intimate terms; Colonel M'Donell's interest was far superior to that of O'Reilly, and had he carried this resolution into effect would no doubt have soon risen to a high rank. The following anecdote of the celebrated Conde de O'Reilly was often related by Colonel M'Donell, as an occurrence which took place at the time both were subalterns, and is evincive of that presence of mind for which Conde was afterwards so eminently distinguished. O'Reilly, having the command of an out picket, was attacked by the Austrians, driven from his post, and left on the field wounded. The Austrians in returning were passing by him, considering him not worthy of notice, when O'Reilly, fearing if left there all night that he might perish, called out, "Were they going to leave the Duke of Alba (then a Spanish General Officer) wounded on the field to perish?" The enemy on hearing this halted, and taking up O'Reilly carried him along with them. As they approached their camp, the rumour that the Duke of Alba was carried in wounded preceded them, on which Count Browne and his whole staff came out to meet their illustrious prisoner. Count Browne on approaching asked if he was the Duke of Alba, was answered "No, I am Mr O'Reilly, Lieutenant in the Irish Brigade, but was obliged to use the stratagem of borrowing the duke's name to prevent my being left on the field to perish."]

(26) John Mackenzie of Torridon, married to Isobel, daughter of Kenneth Mackenzie of Dundonnell. (For notice of him, vide 'History of the Mackenzies.' p.454.)

(27) Glengarry surrendered on 21st August 1746, was sent to Edinburgh Castle and released on 11th October 1749. ('Prisoners of the '45,' vol. iii. p.64.) This visit must therefore have been after 11th October 1749.

Notes

(28) Jean, daughter of Alexander Mackenzie of Davochmaluag.

(29) Dr Ranald of Kylles on Loch Nevis, second son of Alastair Dubh of Glengarry. ('Clan Donald,' vol.iii. p.312.)

(30) Putting aside Cumberland himself, three men have earned special infamy for their brutalities after Culloden. They were Major Lockhart of Cholmondely's Regiment, Captain Carolina Frederick Scott of Guise's Regiment (now the Royal Warwickshire) and Captain John Ferguson of the Navy. This last was the son of William Ferguson, apparently a miller at Insch in Aberdeenshire. In 1746 he was in command of the *Furness* or *Furnace* sloop of War, and the atrocities which he committed fill pages of *The Lyon in Mourning*. In a footnote to p.248 of 'The Origins of the '45' (Scot. Hist. Soc., 2nd Series, vol. ii.) the late Dr W.B. Blaikie writes: "Captain Carolina Frederick Scott shares with Ferguson and Lockhart eternal infamy for superlative cruelty to the hunted Jacobites of the Western Highlands. I find his name and that of Ferguson still perfectly remembered and received with execrations. His Satanic zeal, like Ferguson's, was rewarded with promotion." In both cases, it is said, the promotion was due to the personal intervention of Cumberland.

In 1753, seven years after Culloden, Ferguson is here found in command of the *Porcupine*, and conducting himself in the same way.

(31) [Coll Borisdale's fine stone house of two stories high at Traigh in Knoidart was burnt by this very Captain Ferguson.* At Borisdale, old Borisdale's place, the houses were all burnt, the cattle and other effects of the people taken away by the soldiers. An old woman remarked to the plundering party that although they took all moveables, they could not take away

---

* The house was rebuilt in the 19th century and is known as Inverie House.

the strand which abounded in shell-fish, and upon this party ploughed up the strand; to such a pitch of inveteracy were things carried on. The troops acted in the same manner in other districts.]

(32) Descended from a younger son of Sir James Macdonald, second Baronet of Sleat, John MacDonald obtained a tack of the lands of Totamurich and Knock. His grandson, Ailein-a-Chnuick, was conspicuous for his hostility to the Jacobites after Culloden. He had a commission in one of the independent companies raised in the Hanoverian interest. he married Sibella, daughter of Donald Macleod of Bernera (Mackenzie, 'History of the Macleods,' p.252). He finally settled at Ayr, where he died ('Clan Donald,' vol. iii. p.535), and over his "remains there was placed an inscription not less fulsome than false" (Fraser Mackintosh, 'Antiquarian Notes,' 2nd Series, p. 156).

(33) It seems probable that this was the well-known Captain Arthur Gardiner, who in 1752 was appointed to the *Amazon* frigate "on the Irish station." (Charnock Biog. Navalis, vol. v. p.382.)

(34) Possibly the Hon. Frederick Maitland, son of sixth Earl of Lauderdale. (Vide ib., vol. vi. p.374.)

(35) He became a captain in Fraser's Highlanders, served under Wolfe at the taking of Quebec, and was killed there in 1760. ('Clan Donald,' vol. iii p.341.)

(36) An illegitimate nephew of Colin Campbell of Glenure (the red Fox). He was with his uncle when the latter was shot in the wood of Lettermore on 14th May 1752. He was appointed factor on the forfeited estate of Barrisdale on 10th June 1753.

(37) [Of the M'Donells of Borisdale, a branch of the Glengarry family, there were three generations out in arms for the Stuart cause in 1745 – viz., Archibald M'Donell of Borisdale; Coll, his son; and Archibald, his grandson. Old Archibald had been out twice in arms for the Stuarts before the

Notes

year 1745 – i.e., was at the battle of Shiffermuir or Dumblain, under the Earl of Mar in 1715; and at Killicrankie under Viscount Dundee in 1689. He was a stout and remarkably strong man. In 1745, riding on horseback into Falkirk, in all his arms with his helmet on his head, and his grey locks appearing from under it, he made an awful and respectable appearance. Some strangers seeing him whispered one to another, "Old Glenbucket, by G—d, old Glenbucket, by G—d."]

(38) After Spanish John had gone to America, Black Ronald obtained a tack of certain lands, including Crowlin, whence he was generally known as Raonull Mor a' Chrolen. Details of his adventurous life are given in 'Moidart or Among the Clan Ranalds' (pp. 202 *et seq*) and 'Antiquarian Notes' (2nd Series, p.135). He died 21st November 1813 in his ninety-first year.

(39) His mother was a Nicolson of Scottibreck. ('Clan Donald,' vol. iii p.320.)

(40) Second son of William Macleod of Luskintyre and grandson of Sir Norman Macleod of Bernera. He became a W.S. in 1732, and by his wife Isabel Bannatyne of Kames was father of the judge, Lord Bannatyne.

(41) This George Douglas, Sheriff-Substitute at Fort William, figures in the trial of James of the Glens in 1752.

(42) Alexander Macleod of Ulinish. He was still alive in 1791, and said to be then in his hundredth year. He entertained Johnson and Boswell at Ulinish in 1773.

(43) The name of the lady is not given in the notice of Spanish John in 'Clan Donald,' vol. iii. p.322. But Father Morice says her father was D. M'Donell, killed at Culloden.

www.ingramcontent.com/pod-product-compliance
Lightning Source LLC
LaVergne TN
LVHW051527070426
835507LV00023B/3356